A WALKING TOUR
OF EL PASO, TEXAS

KEN HUDNALL
AND
SHARON HUDNALL

Omega Press
El Paso, Texas

A Walking Tour of El Paso, Texas
COPYRIGHT © 2018 KEN HUDNALL

All rights reserved. No part of this book may be reproduced or transmitted in any form or by any means, graphic, electronic, or mechanical, including photocopying, recording, taping or by any information storage or retrieval system, without the permission in writing from the publisher.

OMEGA PRESS

An imprint of Omega Communications Group, Inc.

For information contact:

Omega Press

5823 N. Mesa, #839

El Paso, Texas 79912

Or http://www.kenhudnall.com

FIRST EDITION

Printed in the United States of America

OTHER WORKS BY THE SAME AUTHOR
FROM OMEGA PRESS

MANHATTAN CONSPIRACY SERIES
Blood on the Apple
Capitol Crimes
Angel of Death
Confrontation

THE OCCULT CONNECTION
UFOs, Secret Societies and Ancient Gods
The Hidden Race
Flying Saucers
UFOs and the Supernatural
UFOs and Secret Societies
UFOs and Ancient Gods
Evidence of Alien Contact
Secrets of Dulce
Intervention
Beyond Roswell
Sensual Alien Encounters

SHADOW WARS
Shadow Rulers

DARKNESS
When Darkness Falls
Fear The Darkness

SPIRITS OF THE BORDER
(with Connie Wang)
The History and Mystery of El Paso Del Norte
The History and Mystery of Fort Bliss, Texas

(with Sharon Hudnall)
The History and Mystery of the Rio Grande
The history and Mystery of New Mexico
The History and Mystery of the Lone Star State
The History and Mystery of Arizona
The History and Mystery of Tombstone, AZ
The History and Mystery of Colorado
Echoes of the Past
El Paso: A City of Secrets
Tales From The Nightshift
The History and Mystery of Sin City
The History and Mystery of Concordia
Military Ghosts
Restless Spirits
School Spirits
Nautical Ghosts
The History and Mystery of San Elizario, Texas
Haunted Hotels
Haunted Hotels in Arizona and Colorado
Ghosts of Tucson
Ghosts of Albuquerque
History and Mystery of Santa Fe and Northern New
Mexico

BOOK OF SECRETS
Ancient Secrets
Secrets of the Dark Web

THE ESTATE SALE MURDERS
Dead Man's Diary

OTHER WORKS

Northwood Conspiracy

No Safe Haven; Homeland Insecurity

Where No Car Has Gone Before

Seventy Years and No Losses:

The History of the Sun Bowl

How Not To Get Published

Vampires, Werewolves and Things
That Go Bump In The Night

Even Paranoids Have Enemies

Criminal Law for Laymen

Understanding Business Law

Language of the Law

Border Escapades of Billy The Kid

PUBLISHED BY PAJA BOOKS
The Occult Connection: Unidentified Flying Objects

DEDICATION

As with all of my books, I could not have completed this book if not for my lovely wife, Sharon.

TABLE OF CONTENTS

PROLOGUE

I guess we should start this volume by making note of the fact that El Paso, Texas is a city that has both a unique history as well as a reputation as being the most haunted city in the country. In these pages we will make an attempt to address both issues.

For over twenty years I have conducted a ghost tour downtown that has fascinated many visitors. I must admit to some puzzlement to discover that many life-long residents of El Paso knew little or nothing about the history of this area. As we discuss many of the buildings in downtown El Paso we will cover both the known history as well as the stories of being haunted.

It should also be remembered that while the area has been inhabited for several hundred years at least, El Paso is not that old a town. In fact, the oldest known image is reproduced here and it only dates to 1850.

Joel Guzman recently discovered this extremely precious image in the John Russell Bartlett Archive of Brown University. It depicts the "Post Opposite Paso del Norte" in approximately December 1850. In those early days, El Paso was known as "Franklin," named after Benjamin Franklin Coons, who leased the adobe buildings you see in the image to the United States Army. The Army occupied the site in the aftermath of the Mexican-American War. The buildings you see here were constructed in the 1830s by Ponce de Leon and once formed the core of his ranch, but Ponce sold them to Coons in 1849. Coons built the corral on the far side of the building in 1850. The civilian population of Franklin at that time was under 100 inhabitants!

The open space in front of the fort is the future San Jacinto Plaza, so the view is to the southwest. A portico would later be added to the main building, which would be demolished in 1883 and replaced by the Grand Central Hotel. Later, Trost's Anson Mills Building (1911) would be erected on the site.

The tallest building in the image, on the south side of the fort, would later be converted into the Central Hotel (not to be confused with the Grand Central Hotel). That happened in 1882. The future "El Paso Street" leads from that structure to the left of the image, from where it led to the river. In those days, the Rio Grande was located approximately where Paisano Dr. is today. The future Segundo Barrio and Chihuahuita were on the south side of the river in Mexico and connected to Paso del Norte (the future Ciudad Juarez)[1].

Original in the John Carter Brown Library at Brown University

Figure 1:Oldest known image of The Post Opposite El Paso Del Norte.

1

El Paso History Alliance added a new photo to El Paso Museum of History's timeline — with Rafael Flores Jr. August 7, 2016

HOTEL PASO DEL NORTE

101 South El Paso Street
El Paso, Texas 79901

Figure 2: Hotel Paso Del Norte (Camino Real Hotel)

The Hotel Paso Del Norte was the dream of Zack T. White, a native of Amherst County, Virginia, who became a very successful El Paso businessman.

Ironically, the design of this historic hotel was the product of two great disasters, the burning of El Paso's Grand Central Hotel in 1892, a well-known four-story structure that had been located on the site of the present-day Mills Building, and the 1906 San Francisco earthquake[2].

The Grand Central Hotel was situated at Pioneer Plaza, at the present site of the Mills building. Opened in 1884, it was owned by J.F. Crosby and Col. Anson Mills and was a modern and elegant hotel. The Grand Central was destroyed by fire on Feb. 11, 1892.

Figure 3: Grand Central Hotel

According to the story, the Grand Central Hotel was basically a cattleman's hotel. Cattle was bought and sold in the lobby between cattlemen and representatives of

---

[2] Jones, Harriot Howze, El Paso: A Centennial Report, A Project of the El Paso County Historical Society, Superior Printing Inc, Texas 1972.

processing companies. One night in 1892, the hotel was full and business was brisk, Late one night, the hotel caught on fire due to unknown causes. When guests arrived at the exists, it was found that the doors were chained shut. Many on the upper floors retreated to the rooms in hopes of escaping the fire. Unfortunately, many of those perished either from the flames or the thick smoke.

Among the many who gathered to watch the fire was a prominent El Paso business man by the name of Zack T, White. Zack T. White was one of those who had actively helped try to extinguish the fire at the Grand Central Hotel and recalled this incident as the beginning of his idea to build a modern fire proof hotel in El Paso[3].

In spite of his dream to build a state of the art hotel, it was not a dream to be quickly realized. It took something as traumatic as a major earthquake to galvanize White to move forward with his plan. After the 1906 San Francisco earthquake, Zack White and J.E. Lewis, an engineer, went to San Francisco to study the buildings that survived he earthquake and the ensuing firestorms. After a detailed examination of those buildings that survived, they copied the foundation plans and the design features of those buildings that had survived the quake. These earthquake

---

[3] Ibid

proof features coupled with a fireproof design were incorporated into the plans drawn up for the Hotel Paso Del Norte (the Hotel on the Pass to the North), which opened for guests in December 1912.

Of course, the Paso Del Norte was not White's only contribution to El Paso. He aided in the building of the first Santa Fe Street International Bridge, which was replaced by the Paso Del Norte Bridge in 1967. He helped build the first brick plant in El Paso as well as the first streetcar line. He served as Vice President of the Gas, Electric Light and Power Company. He was one of El Paso's strongest advocates for the use of electricity and gas. But he is most remembered for the building of his "dream hotel."

The Hotel Paso del Norte was built on the site formerly occupied by the Kohlberg Cigar Store and Factory[4], the Guarantee Shoe Store and the Happy Hour

---

[4] Built up by Ernst Kohlberg and his brother, the factory was originally located on El Paso Street, it moved to Santa Fe Street in 1911. A lot of skilled Mexican workers were employed there. Ernst Kohlberg (1857–1910) was born in Beverungen, Westphalia, at that time a province of Prussia. He left home in 1875 with Solomon C. Schutz, who had business interests in the El Paso area. Kohlberg agreed to work for Schutz without salary for six months to a year in order to defray the costs of his passage to Texas. The two reached Franklin, as El Paso was then called, by stagecoach. After working off his debt to Schutz, Kohlberg invested in a Mexican gold mine and worked in San Francisco before returning to Franklin in 1881 and opening a cigar store in partnership with his brother. On a family visit to Germany in 1884, Kohlberg met and married Olga Bernstein. The two became

Theatre, El Paso's best known vaudeville house. It took two years for the 1.5 million dollar building to be completed by Trost and Trost Architects[5] and J.E. Lewis, the construction engineer. Only the finest materials were used in the construction of Mr. White's "dream hotel" as he desired that the hotel would be the finest constructed building in El Paso at the time and for many years to come. The ten-story structure was built of steel and concrete on an earthquake-proof foundation, with a brick exterior and terra cotta trim. The inside partitions and walls were made from "fire-proof" white gypsum from nearby White Sands.

The lobby was designed with a meticulous attention to detail, Mr. White had Italian artisans brought to El Paso to do the work he wanted. He had Tiffany's of New York

---

prominent civic leaders and philanthropists in El Paso; Olga Kohlberg founded the first public kindergarten in Texas. The Kohlbergs were successful business entrepreneurs who made valuable and memorable civic contributions to the development of El Paso and West Texas. In 1886 the Kohlberg brothers established the first cigar factory in the Southwest. They operated the business under the name of Kohlberg Brothers Tobacco Company. Five years later, the young businessmen opened the International Cigar Factory. As the first cigar manufacturers in the Southwest area, the Kohlbergs' signature product became the popular La Internacional cigar.

Among Ernst Kohlberg's other holdings was the St. Charles Hotel, which he leased to a compulsive gambler who in 1910 shot and killed Kohlberg after falling far behind in his rent. Mr. and Mrs. Kohlberg had four children, three boys and one girl. Olga Kohlberg died in 1935.

[5] Englebrecht, Lloyd C. and June-Marie, Henry C. Trost, Architect of the Southwest, El Paso Public Library Associates, 1981.

specially design and construct the golden Tiffany stained glass dome with its elaborate mahogany carvings that graces the lobby of this grand old hotel. The dome is actually made up of seventeen pieces and is suspended by wires due to the tremendous weight, which would otherwise collapse in the center.

The Dome Bar Chandeliers are unique in their design. During one of the renovations of the hotel, these European chandeliers were installed to light the lobby. These electrically lit fixtures were among the first electrical lights in the area. The chandeliers in the Dome Restaurant, which was originally called The Depot, are replicas of the original candle chandeliers that were lowered in the evening for the candles to be lit and then raised back to their normal height. There were actually three lobbies in the original design, each decorated with cherry stone, green and golden scagiola, lit by European chandeliers and trimmed with black, serpentine marble. It was truly the finest hotel of its type in the country. This showplace opened on Thanksgiving Day of the year 1912 with a very lavish ball.

Over the years the roof top ballroom and patio were the scenes of many dinner dances and Sunday tea dances. It was also the preferred gathering place for those who wanted to watch the progress of Poncho Villa's forces across the river in Juarez during the Mexican Revolution. Later is became the center of the cattle industry, with more cattle being bought and sold in the lobby of this hotel than any other single location in the world.

This historic old hotel remained in the White family until 1970 when TGK Investment Co., Ltd. bought the structure from Mary and Katherine White, the daughters of Zack T. White. There have been several renovations and remodelings of the Hotel Paso Del Norte, the most recent major change being the addition of the 17-story tower in 1986.

Zack White wanted to build the most modern hotel in the southwest. Therefore, on December 19, 1912, he had a huge oil storage tank installed in the Hotel Paso Del Norte[6]. The tank, manufactured by the El Paso Foundry, was 8 feet in diameter and 62 feet long. It was constructed to hold 12,100 gallons of oil to be used for heating the hotel. The plan was for the tank to be filled directly from railroad tank cars on the G.H. & S.A. tracks through a pipeline built directly to the hotel.

---

[6] From an unpublished history of the Camino Real Hotel loaned to the author.

The original hotel used coal to fire the boilers that provided steam heat to the rooms. The coal would be collected in rail cars and dumped on the yard adjacent to the property. In 1915, the Hotel Paso Del Norte built a coal bin underneath the hotel in which the coal would be placed instead of leaving it out in the weather. Interestingly enough, the coal bin was built next to the hotel bakery.

The original design of the hotel did not have closets in the rooms. Instead, guests would use cloakrooms with hooks mounted on the walls to hold their clothing. This was done because in those days, most travelers would carry their clothing rolled up in large carpet bags. When the traveler would arrive at their destination, they would unroll the garments and hang them on hooks. This is why the rooms in the old section of the hotel offer mahogany armoires instead of closets for the use of the guests. There is no question that Zack White spared no expense in ensuring that the Paso Del Norte was a thoroughly modern hotel. Another unusual feature of this magnificent hotel was the installing in the basement of tiled hot tubs and bathing areas for use by the guests.

Of course, I am sure that Mr. White had no plans for his hotel to become a haven for the restless spirits of those who have not yet gone on to wherever it is that the dead go, however, almost from the first, guests, employees and staff have seen and heard things that are beyond the ordinary and the expected. I am told that some people refuse to stay in the old sections of the hotel due to unusual occurrences.

I have attended many events that this historic old hotel, and naturally, in idle discussion with other attendees at these various functions, the conversation has often turned to the stories association with the old hotel. For example, I heard that a young woman wearing a long white dress has been seen in the basement of this hotel, by members of the staff.

According to the story associated with this ghost girl, she had gotten pregnant and thus it was agreed that she and her young man would get married. As both families were somewhat prominent in the community, arrangements were made that this wedding, that was to take place on the tenth floor of the hotel, would be one of the first events to take place at the newly completed Hotel Paso del Norte. The wedding was apparently the social event of the season and everyone looked forward to it, especially the pregnant girl. When the big day arrived, everyone was at the hotel, except the groom. He never showed up. Mortified and depressed at being left at the altar, the young would-be bride jumped to her death from one of the tenth floor windows. It is said that it is her spirit that comes back looking for her young man. This author met her in the elevator and she looked as real as can be.

On the mezzanine, is has been said that sometimes, usually late at night or in the early hours of the new day, members of the cleaning crew will see a door where there has not been a door before. When they get close to the mysterious door and listen, the sounds of a party can be clearly heard coming from behind the door. No one, as of yet, I am told, has opened the door to see what is beyond it. Rather, those who say they have seen the mysterious door have gone to get someone else to witness this rather bizarre situation. When they return, the door and the sounds emanating from behind it have vanished. They find only blank wall where the door had been only a short time before. Perhaps, one day, someone will have the courage to jerk open that mysterious door and see what is lurking behind it – or will they?

Zack T. White's original Hotel Paso del Norte has been added onto several times over the years. The current entrance and Registration Desk is in the new addition. In 1986, the Dome Bar was built, directly beneath the exquisite Tiffany Dome for which the hotel is so known.

As a result of this conversion of the lobby area into a bar, the original entrance to the hotel now opens directly into the Dome Bar and is rarely used. Another of the expansions to the original Hotel Paso del Norte resulted in the demolishing of the Ellanay Theater, a historic old theater that had been built in 1918, by J.M. Lewis and Victor Andreas, at the cost of $94,500.00. The Ellanay opened to great fanfare on November 10, 1918 with a seating capacity of 940.

Many came to the Ellanay just to see the unbelievably ornate façade. The two owners had spared no expense in trying to outdo all of the other similar enterprises in the city. There was a recessed arch over the marquee that enclosed a glazed tile mural featuring three muses from Greek mythology and two paired couples dressed in Roman clothing. Tree foliage formed the foreground under the arch and a Renaissance landscape in the background completed the eye-catching mural. The figures and the foreground were in bas-relief. The glazed tiles were large, about 24" square. The entire arch was approximately 25' in length. About four feet below the cornice of the building were busts of J.M. Lewis and Victor Andreas. Unfortunately, the 1983 expansion of the Hotel

Paso del Norte resulted in the destruction of this beautiful old building.

There is another entrance into what used to be the original Hotel Paso Del Norte Bar, now called Uptowns, from San Antonio Street that is also almost always locked. As a result, the historic original bar, which sometimes is opened for parties and political events, is seldom used.

At one event my wife and I attended at the hotel, which is now known as the Camino Real Hotel, we were early and the doors to the ballroom on the Mezzanine, where the event was to be held, were still locked so the staff would finish setting up the room. So we went to the Dome Bar to wait. While we were sitting there, I idly asked the cocktail waitress about a story I had heard of people walking out of the wall in the lobby. She smiled for a moment and looked around the bar. We were early enough that there weren't too many people about, so she balanced her tray against one hip and told us the following story:

"Well, I heard that there is a mural on the wall showing a group of people standing around a piano." I had never really noticed the mural before, I have to admit; however, I have two friends who tell me that they have seen the mural the young lady was referring to.

"I heard that one night," she went on in a lower voice, "one of the night managers was checking the bar, and comparing sales against stock levels, things like that. He began to feel like something was wrong and he glanced up to see a woman walk out of the mural and stop in the middle of the floor. He described her as young, slim and attractive. She was dressed in clothing from years ago and he said she was wearing one of those big hats with flowers on it. The woman looked around like she was confused or something and never seemed to notice the night manager standing only a few feet away. He went around the bar and started toward her, but she backed up right into that mural. He went over and ran his hands over the wall, but there was no place she could have gone. He suddenly remembered a job he had to do elsewhere and left the bar."

I asked if she had been seen again, and the young lady said it was rumored that some of the housekeeping staff had seen her once or twice walk out of the mural, but they had rarely stayed to see what the lady did after that. More than one worker, she said, had quit after seeing some of the things that happened in the hotel. She had not personally witnessed anything, but still, she heard a lot of stories that made her a little afraid to work the night shift in the bar.

Deciding to see if I could verify the stories that I had heard, I went to the hotel and asked to speak to the manager. I was directed to a lovely young lady by the name of Michelle L. Kaip, CMP, who is the Director of Sales. She very kindly took time out of her busy schedule to tell me the stories that she had heard since coming to the Camino Real.

I frankly expected a blanket denial that there were any ghosts at the Camino Real Hotel, however, Ms. Kaip was very frank with me. She said that she has heard folklore concerning two prominent spirits who have appeared from time to time at the property. The best known story, she said was about a young woman in a white gown. According to what she had been told, the girl was to be married at the Hotel Paso Del Norte but something happened and now she haunts the 10th floor. I asked if she had any idea of the name of the ghost and she said that it was rumored to be Katherine White, daughter of Zack T, White.

The other spirit that seemed to frequent the hotel is a well-dressed man who wears a black suit cut in the style of the 19th century and always wears a bowler hat. This figure has been seen a number of time and is rumored to be

Ben S. Dowell, a Kentuckian, which became El Paso's first mayor. She added that Ben Dowell's home and saloon stood at 115 S. El Paso Street, coincidentally, the spot where the Hotel Paso Del Norte's original bar was built. I asked for examples of his appearances and she said that she had heard from housekeeping that he has the habit of appearing in closets and other odd places, scaring the daylights out of the housekeeper who comes upon him unexpectedly.

I asked about the stories that I had heard about doors suddenly appearing on the Mezzanine Level. She said that she had heard from Housekeeping that unexplained doorways and stairways have appeared at different locations throughout the hotel where there may have once been a door or stairway that does not exist today. She had not heard the story that I related to her of a housekeeper hearing a party going on behind one of the closed doors.

I then asked about the mural around the Dome Bar where the lady allegedly walked out of the wall. She replied that she knew of a large photograph but not a mural in the bar area. She said that there is faded artwork in what was the 10th floor ballroom, but she could not think of any murals in the lobby area.

I asked about seeing the artwork in the ballroom and she replied that it was no longer open to the public as what was the original ballroom is now an engineering room. Talking of the engineering department reminded her of a story that a friend had told her. She said that this was a man she knew well who had worked in the Engineering Department. He had been in the Dome Bar one day when the man in the bowler hat came into the bar and sat down beside him. Her friend said that they had a very nice conversation of some length. He seriously thought he was talking to a guest until the man in the bowler hat had gotten up from his seat, walked into the corner near the bar and vanished. She was very confident that he was a credible witness.

I asked about other stories she had heard since joining the staff and she said that most of them dealt with occurrences on the 10th floor or in the lobby, though, as she had mentioned earlier in our conversation, the housekeepers talk of the man with the bowler hat appearing in various places around the hotel.

In retrospect, it is not a wild notion to think that the Hotel Paso Del Hotel, or the Camino Real, to call it by its' current name, could or would be haunted. Much life and death in El Paso over the almost one hundred years the hotel has stood has been associated with this imposing structure. Due to its' location, the Hotel Paso Del Norte was the virtual center of life in early El Paso. The photograph below is a re-enactment done in 1966 of the April 14, 1881 famous "Four Men Shot Dead in Five Seconds"

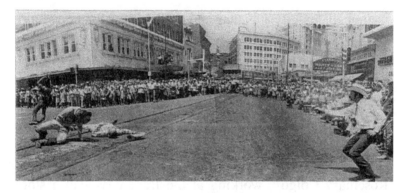

Figure 4: Location of the shootout that left 5 men dead in 5 seconds
shootout took place in front of the Hotel Paso Del Norte. In this confrontation, Dallas Stoudenmire, the newly appointed city marshal, was called upon to deal with the murder of a former Texas Ranger named Krempkau by Johnny Hale, manager of the Manning's' ranch and a man on trial already for the murder of two Mexicans. Some of the testimony at the trial had been in Spanish and Krempkau had acted as translator for the court. Hale didn't like what was said and chose to accost Krempkau during

the noon recess with a hidden gun that had been smuggled to him by friends.

So in this famous shootout, Johnny Hale killed Krempkau. Stoudenmire pulled his weapons and shot at Hale, but killing a man named Lopez, an innocent bystander. Then he fired again and killed Hale. George Campbell, ex-city marshal and an enemy of Stoudenmire chose to draw on the marshal. Stoudenmire killed Campbell. Of such confusion, legends are made and the death of an innocent man is forgotten.

Ms. Kaip graciously allowed me to wander the hotel and talk to some of the staff. A very cute young lady, Rosemary Coigoy, working at the front desk had a story about a guest staying on the 16th floor, directly below the Presidential Suite on the 17th floor. She was working the graveyard shift one night and the guest called to complain that the noisy party and the loud piano music coming from the floor above were keeping him awake. Security was dispatched to the suite, but it was empty, there was no party and no one was playing the Grand Piano in the Presidential Suite. However, at the same time, in the room below the sounds of the party could still be heard.

I then talked to Robert Diaz, Director of Security for the Hotel. He related two incidents that he had been involved in during his time on the job. A new manager that had been transferred to El Paso was living in the Hotel while looking for a house. One afternoon, she and her daughter went to the pool on the 10th floor. Upon her arrival at the pool, she saw someone she thought was suspicious, a lady who appeared extremely angry. She stood outside the only door to the pool area and called down to Security. Two officers were dispatched to check on the lady. When they arrived there was no one in the pool area. Assuming that she may have gotten out and left by way of the stairs, they checked the stairs all the way to the street level but never found anyone. She could not have gotten out of the pool area without being seen.

The other incident happened during the construction of the new floors. There was night security furnished by the contractor to make sure that the tools were safe. One night he was called by Hotel Security personnel and told that the security furnished by the contractor had run off of the job and that one man had kept running in he got to the street. They were unable to find that particular man who had been the one to spark the panic.

Finally, the guard that had disappeared was found and questioned. He said that his job had been to provide security for the seventeenth floor. He said that he was been warned not to shut the doors along the hall as they had all just been painted and it was fear that they would stick shut. Workers' tools were stored in several rooms so he was to just sit in the hallway and make sure that no one got into the rooms and stole any of the tools. He said that he had been sitting by a window reading a book when one of the doors, being held open by a doorstop, suddenly slammed shut. He got up, opened the door and replaced the doorstop and then went back to his book.

In a few minutes, he glanced back up to see the doorstop from one of the doors slide across the floor and that door slammed shut. Curious, thinking a friend might be playing a joke on him he reopened the door, replaced the doorstop and searched the entire floor, but found no one. He went back to his book and all was peaceful for a few minutes and then in unison, every door slammed shut. At that point he had panicked, and run screaming down the stairs. The guard on the sixteenth floor had heard him run by and he started running down the stairs behind him and then the guard on the fifteenth floor also started to run behind them. All he knew for sure was that he was not going back in that building.

In another incident, it seems during the construction in the 1990s, a crane fell from the roof, taking a worker along with it. The crane and the worker had crashed into the roof of the third floor. The only way to get the dead worker off of the roof of the third floor was to take him through one of the guest rooms. From that time forth, no one wants to stay in that room and from time to time, those in the offices in the part of the third floors where the crane crashed will hear something slam into the roof above them.

Finally, there is the story of Alice, a young lady who is said to have died in the hotel. When I wrote the book entitled Haunted Hotels, I was furnished with a photo taken by the night manager of the 4th floor. He said that he stepped off of the elevator to see Alice walking down the hallway. He immediately snapped a photo with his cell phone and then later sent it to me. In the photo the little girl is carrying a doll.

In 2015, I was told, the staff had put up a memorial to Alice on the 6th floor on the Day of the Dead. As a final touch, they had placed a Barbie on the memorial. When they went to dismantle the memorial on November 2nd the doll was gone. She was carrying the missing doll in the photo snapped by the manager.

There is a room on the 6th floor that seems to be a favorite of young Alice. Upon entering the room, the atmosphere is like stepping into a freezer. Many guests occupying their room have awoken to see her hovering over the bed. Needless to say many of these guests vacated the hotel immediately.

But there is one final interesting point. A number of employees in the restaurant have told of receiving room service calls from their room. Upon arriving, the room is normally found to be empty. Perhaps Alice just wants a little attention.

THE PLAZA THEATRE

125 Pioneer Plaza
El Paso, Texas

Figure 5: The Plaza theater

Prior to the Plaza Theatre being built, there had been a large produce warehouse, belonging to Bernard and Ben Schuster, which occupied the location on Pioneer Plaza. In 1927 the Plaza was constructed.

Over Fifty years ago, El Pasoans would line the streets waiting to enter the theater to follow the adventures of heroes and be swept up in tearful romances. The Plaza Theater was the center of El Paso's entertainment and everyone looked forward to the appearance of a new movie on the brightly lit marquee. It was a place of excitement and where young lovers could hold hands and more in the dimly lit interior. The smell of freshly popped corn was in the air and soft drinks just tasted better bought from the theater's soda fountain. This land of enchantment and beauty was the ornately designed Plaza Theater of fifty years ago.

Unfortunately, all things must end and what is fascinating to us today is boring tomorrow. A few short years ago, you could walk down the same streets and not even know the Plaza Theater exists. No longer did crowds of excited young people jostle each other to get the best seats, the marquee is no longer lit. The silver screen was dark and nothing moved in the darkened building. Except as we shall see, perhaps the theater is not as deserted as it first appears. The once beautiful and intriguing Plaza Theater had its doors closed for over twenty years before it was decided to resurrect the historic old structure. It was and still is one of the few theaters of its kind in this country.

Nearly 90 years ago, Louis L. Dent, owner of the principal El Paso theaters at the time, decided to buy the property on Pioneer Plaza, then occupied by The Herald News. Dent was a man who wanted to give back to a city that had done so much for him. As he said in the El Paso Times in February of 1927, "El Paso has been good to me, and I am going to put something everybody will proud of."

To achieve his dream, Louis Dent contracted with H.T. Ponsford & Sons to build a theater unlike anything anyone had heard of before. Architect W. Scott Dunne prepared the Spanish Colonial architectural style and C.A. Goetting Construction Company erected this unique building, beginning construction of the Plaza Theater in 1929.

From September 12, 1930 when the Plaza Theater first opened its doors, it fascinated El Pasoans and people from other areas with its uniqueness and glamour. Patrons went to the popular Plaza to be seen as much as to see the entertainment. It was known as "The Greatest Showplace in the Southwest," home to a multitude of elegant and lavish decorations.

Valuable oil paintings, antiques and other art objects found their home throughout the lobbies, halls and stairways of the theater. Posh carpeting, wrought iron banisters and mosaic tile floors and walls adorned the lobby and foyer. The building itself, along with its furnishings, was of elegant Spanish motif.

The extravagance of the Plaza's architectural design held fast, from its transition from a theater for live stage performances, to a theater exhibiting first-run motion pictures.

At the point where the entrance wing of the Plaza adjoined the auditorium, a domed tower rose in three tiers, projecting above the roof line. Other exterior references to the style included modest brick delineations at the building's corners, simple cartouche motifs and stepped and curved parapets with tile accents along the roof line. All these exquisite styles suited our city perfectly.

Among the best known features of the Plaza was its Wurlitzer organ, played before live performances and movies and during intermissions. Resting below the actual seating area in front of the stage and out of the audience's view, the organ was elevated to its playing position, astonishing theater goers. After a musical interlude, the organ was lowered back to its original position on the platform.

The organ had 15 ranks with 61 pipes in each rank. It originally cost about $60,000. This elegant organ is one thing that many El Pasoans seem to remember most. Unfortunately, it was removed and sold to an organ collector in 1972.

The Plaza was by far the most elaborate and modern theater of its kind, boasting many new and innovative features, among them the first refrigerated air conditioning in the United States. This technology not only cooled the air in the summer but warmed it in the winter.

The Plaza could accommodate more than 2,000 people comfortably. The original seating capacity was 2,410, with 1,510 seats on the main floor, 508 in the mezzanine and 392 in the balcony. Patrons would meet and mingle inside the Plaza, while above them in the auditorium puffy clouds crossed a sky filled with twinkling stars. Two machines worth $1,500 each controlled the enchanted sky.

John Wayne, Ethyl Barrymore, Mae West and Joan Crawford, among others, performed live at the Plaza during the height of their popularity. On February 10, 1934, the Plaza's very first stage drama, "Richelieu," was performed for El Pasoans. The cast included the then famous Walter Hampton, Dallas Anderson, John Davenport and Mable More. Other memorable plays presented at the Plaza were "The Taming of the Shrew" and the "The Little Foxes."

During the Plaza's heyday, motorists and pedestrians going down San Francisco and El Paso streets could see the grand old theater for blocks. With its brilliantly lighted marquee announcing another production, the Plaza was a sight to behold. The Plaza hosted the world premiere of the film "El Paso," which drew a capacity and star-studded crowd, and also showed Tom Lea's popular "The Brave Bulls."

Parents and grandparents of today's generation once experienced the Plaza that emphasized our city's cultural beauty. Most El Pasoans who grew up here will have a story or two to tell about the Plaza. Many people had their first date there or their first kiss while waiting for the curtain to rise. It was a place where sweet memories were made. Because of its historical importance to our area, the Plaza has been named a Historical Landmark by the

National Register. Peter Flagg Maxon, Chief Architectural Historian of the Texas Historical Commission, states, "We believe the Plaza Theater to be one of the most significant architecturally and historically in the state of Texas."

The above is the accepted history and the current activities to preserve this wonderful old building. But from the many stories that I have heard, it would seem that there are a number of others who have a much more direct interest in having the Plaza preserved. I am referring, of course to the many spirits that are said to still inhabit the monument to a lost age of innocence and glamour.

Turning once again to the interview given by Dr. John O. West to the El Paso Times[7], he maintained that the oldest story of hauntings at this location stems from colonial days, when El Paso was a part of Mexico. It seems that a wealthy Spaniard built a mansion on the location where the Plaza now sits for his beautiful wife. The exquisite mansion was built some distance from the settlement of Paso De Norte. It seems that the husband was very jealous and due to the beauty of his wife, was afraid that she would fall in love with someone else and leave

---

[7]Fennell, Molly, *Ghosts: Professor Recalls Strange Tales From Past*, El Paso Times, October 24, 1962.

him. The poor woman spent her days inside the mansion, usually tending her flowers in the garden.

Though the wife was very faithful to her husband and tried to do nothing to anger him, his unreasonable jealousy continued to cause problems between them. On one occasion, enraged at his wife, the jealous husband strangled her. When he calmed down, realizing that he had killed the love of his life, the husband burned the beautiful mansion to the ground and rode away, never to be seen again.

Many visitors to the plaza have seen a woman walking on a balcony that can only be reached by a ladder – of course there is no ladder. This woman, said by others to be wearing clothing such as was worn by the wealthy in colonial days, spends her time trying to water the plastic flowers that are used to decorate the balcony.

The story widely told of a spirit in the Plaza Theater concerns a man who went to the Theater to see a show. During intermission, he got up and went to get a drink, but just short of the drinking fountain, he had a massive heart attack and died. It is said that his ghost roams the hallway, still looking for that drink of water.

There is still another story, which may actually be a variation of the story of the ghost hunting for that drink of water, but this one involves a soldier from Fort Bliss that died of a heart attack while smoking in the men's room. There have been a number of reports of a man dressed in a military uniform that has been seen on the right side of the stairs smoking a cigarette. There have also been a number of reports of sounds like someone choking coming from the basement.

There is also a story that was in Haunted El Paso[8] of a worker needing to bring some heavy equipment up from the basement. Grabbing the front of the heavy load, the worker dug in his heels, dragging the heavy equipment to the steps. Painfully, he then stated trying to lift it up each step. Finally, one of the carpenters who had been working in the basement came over, lifted the lower end of the burden and helped carry it to the top of the stairs. When the worker who had been assigned the job turned to thank the Good Samaritan who had helped him, there was no one there.

This theater was not the only theater that El Paso had at the time. In the same time that the Plaza opened another the theater opened, this one was the Festival Theater. This one was a semi pro theater. The both of them

---

[8] Chapman, Christine, _Haunted El Paso_, Looking at El Paso, Vol.3, No. 5, October 29 to November 11, 1999.

were had the purpose to serve the people of El Paso. Even though the Festival Theater was a non-profit, the Plaza was not. The Festival Theater was run by the donations of the wealthy people who would go. They are both very old, however the Plaza one is much older. It opened in the 1910s and became a land mark for El Paso and the Texas state and love it very much.

In 1929, construction of the **Spanish Colonial Revival style** Plaza Theater began. It was designed by the prolific Dallas architect W. Scott Dunne, who is credited with more than 30 theaters in Texas and Oklahoma. Today the Plaza is recognized as his surviving masterpiece. H. Ponsford & Sons built the theater, which was constructed by C.A. Goetting Construction Company. The Plaza was designed, as a modern film house in a Spanish Colonial revival style with the flexibility of presenting stage shows. Construction was completed in 1930. **The Wurlitzer Company installed a $60,000 pipe organ. It was advertised as the "largest theater of its kind between Dallas and Los Angeles."**

Opening night was on September 12, 1930 with the movie "Follow Through" to a capacity crowd of 2,410. Although several theaters existed in downtown El Paso at the time the Plaza Theatre opened, its size, elaborate decor, and technical innovations made it stand out. It was advertised as the largest theater of its kind between Dallas and Los Angeles. The Plaza has been a vaudeville or burlesque house as well as also showing movies. The theater featured an "atmospheric" ceiling complete with twinkling stars which were astronomically correct stars and projections of lazily floating clouds. It was the first public theater in the United States with air conditioning.

In 1933, Interstate Theaters purchased the Plaza Theatre.[3] On February 10, 1934, the Plaza's very first stage drama, *Richelieu*, was performed. The cast included then famous Walter Hampton, Dallas Anderson, John Davenport and Mable More. In 1939, the theater showed *Gone With the Wind* in two different showings because of Jim Crow laws in El Paso. The first showing was whites only, but a civil rights activist, Betty Mary Goetting, prevailed on the Plaza Theatre to show a midnight screening which African Americans could attend. The midnight showing of *Gone With the Wind* was reported to be "packed." In 1949, the Plaza hosted the world premiere of the film "El Paso," which drew a capacity and star-studded crowd, and also showed Tom Lea's "The Brave Bulls."

Decline

By the 1950s, two major influences factored into a slow decline in the Plaza Theatre's patronage. The advent of television and the rise of suburban neighborhoods located farther and farther away from downtown served as major challenges to the Plaza Theatre in addition to other downtown establishments.[2][3] At the same time, a new source of competition arose with the advent of drive-in theaters in the late 1940s.

By the early 1970s, the theater had fallen into disrepair, and was sold. Many of its impressive amenities, including furnishings, artwork, and the Mighty Wurlitzer Organ were auctioned off. Only by the acquisition of the theater by the local Dipp Family in 1973 was the Plaza saved from demolition at that time.

The Plaza closed on May 31, 1974. In 1985, the state of Texas declared the Plaza Theatre to be a Historical Landmark. It was briefly reopened in 1970 and 1980, only to finally close its doors in 1989.

In 1989, after years of infrequent programming, the decision was made to demolish the Plaza Theatre in order to make way for a parking lot. Spurred by a groundswell of community support, the El Paso Community Foundation began negotiations to raise the required $9 million to save the theater from demolition. With only six weeks to raise the funds, fundraising events were held across the community with the most visible effort being staged by actress Rita Moreno the day before the deadline. It was announced that evening that enough money had been raised to save the Plaza Theatre. After the El Paso Community Foundation placed a new roof on the theater, it was donated to the City of El Paso in 1990. Even though this theater was falling it was still trying to pull itself up.

Reopening

One of the few remaining theaters of its kind in the country, the Plaza had lost most of its original splendor. Furnishings and artwork had been removed, the facade had been altered, and parts of its once-advanced electrical systems were no longer functional, yet the interior structure appeared as it had for close to seventy years. In 2000, a volunteer steering committee, assembled by the El Paso Community Foundation, began to assess the viability of restoring the Plaza Theatre. The committee concluded that the project was feasible, and in 2001, a leading promoter, producer and marketer of live entertainment events, conducted an extensive survey of El Paso's local performing arts community. The survey concluded that: a market did exist in El Paso for additional performing arts programming, and that the public had a strong affinity for the Plaza and was eager to attend events at a restored Plaza.

On July 30, 2002 the City of El Paso formally approved a public/private partnership with the El Paso Community Foundation to restore the Plaza Theatre to its original appearance. The Foundation committed to raising $12 million towards the renovation effort, to restoring and reinstalling the Mighty Wurlitzer Organ at the Plaza Theatre, and to donating the adjacent building (Centre Annex), which would be integrated into the overall operations of the Plaza. The City of El Paso agreed to fund the remaining cost of the restoration.

Thos. S. Byrne, Ltd. and Arrow Builders were hired to perform the restoration. The companies took particular interest in the project, noting that "With over 2,000 seats at the commencement of restoration, the Plaza is currently one of the nation's largest non-functioning theaters in the United States." The companies worked diligently to insure all phases of construction complied with historical restoration guidelines.

At a cost of nearly $38 million, the Plaza reopened on March 17, 2006.[2] The first performance hosted at the refurbished theater was **River Dance** which played Friday, March 17, 2006 through Sunday, March 19 with multiple sold-out performances. The reopened theater boasts a 2,050-seat main theater with a 10-story stage house capable of handling large traveling Broadway shows. In addition, with the completion of the Centre Annex, the facility includes a 200-seat children's theater, a rooftop garden, meeting facilities and a privately managed restaurant. The smaller theater is named the Philanthropy Theatre.

Despite the completion of the project, the El Paso Community Foundation continues appropriating funds to buy back original art and furnishings of the Plaza.

No expense was spared in creating the elaborate building. At the point where the entrance wing of the Plaza adjoined the auditorium, a domed tower rises in three tiers, projecting above the roof line. Other exterior references to the Spanish mission-style included modest brick delineations at the building's corners, simple cartouche motifs and stepped and curved parapets with tile accents along the roof line. While the exterior facade was designed to be reminiscent of a mission-style parapet, patrons were awed by the interior, with its intricately painted ceilings, mosaic-tiled floors, Posh carpeting, decorative wrought iron banisters and sconces and, to heighten the effect, antique furnishings. Due to such grandiose rococo design, the Plaza became known as "The Showplace of the Southwest."

The Mighty Wurlitzer

Further emphasis of the illustrious interior stands in the $60,000 Mighty Wurlitzer Organ, designed to elevate from the orchestra pit to accompany vaudeville shows, sing-alongs, and to entertain patrons before and after films. Its "toy box" provides the organ with the versatility to replicate such sounds as horses' hooves, the ocean surf and birds chirping. The organ had 15 ranks with 61 pipes in each rank.

In 1973, the Mighty Wurlitzer Organ was sold at auction and housed at the home of a private collector in Dallas. In 1998 the organ was restored and returned to El Paso as a donation by the late Karl O. Wyler, Sr. During renovations of the theater, the organ was put on display at Sunland Park Mall located in Northwest El Paso The organ was rebuilt by Pipe Organ Artisans of Arizona, Tucson, and re-installed. The Opus 2123 console was returned to its original finish. It is the only one of its kind (a Wurlitzer Balaban III) left intact.[7]

THE WHITE HOUSE

Figure 6: Early Photo of the Central Hotel

The building long known as the White House is the latest of a series of structures to stand on the location it currently occupies. The original building was also known as the La Casa Blanca or The Centre. It was a Sullivanesque department store & hotel, designed by Henry C. Trost[9], Trost & Trost, El Paso. The supervising architect was New York-born John J. Stewart[10]. The building was constructed by builder Felix Martinez. The store originally

---

[9] 1860-1933
[10] 1847-1928

occupied the 1st floor, basement & probably the mezzanine while the remaining floors were occupied by the hotel.

A 1917 store addition extended the originally shortened 3rd - 5th floors to match the length of the building. The annex later increased to 7 floors

The following history was gleaned from articles in the El Paso Times,

Tracing its ancestry back to 1880, the White House Department Store has given El Paso and Juarez more than three quarters of a century of service.

Father of the big establishment was Felix Brunschwig who, with his uncle, established the "City of London" store in Juarez in 1880.

Brunschwig and his uncle were emigrants from Alsace-Lorraine.

Deciding El Paso held a bigger future than Juarez, Brunschwig closed the "City of London" in June, 1990, and established the White House in El Paso in September the same year.

First location of the White House was at San Antonio and Oregon Streets, presently occupied by Union Fashion.

Only 10 employees staffed the first White House, although it was a larger-than-average store even then.

One of the earliest employees to go to work in the store was Jake Miller, who took a job as delivery boy in 1900 and worked his way up to the presidency of the firm.

FIRM INCORPORATED

In 1903 the White House was incorporated and in 1908 two nephews of Brunschwig's, Gaston and Myrtil Coblentz, became chief owners of the store, which was more of a specialty shop than a department store.

Deciding on expansion, to keep up with the growth of El Paso, the owners obtained the present Pioneer Plaza site and constructed the first part of the present White House building, completing it in 1915.

That initial store was of modest size compared to the present large White House installation. It consisted of only a basement, main floor and mezzanine. The basement was used chiefly as a stockroom, but was converted into a selling floor in 1914.

Myrtil Coblentz became president of the company in 1915 and more expansion was soon undertaken.

The second, third and fourth floors were added in 1917 and the White House branched out into a full-fledged department store, giving up its role as a specialty shop.

Founder of the firm, Felix Brunschwig, died in Paris, France, in 1922.

In 1923 more expansion became necessary and the fifth floor was added. An early example of the company's good employee relations was evident that year, also, when the employees' lunchroom was opened for use.

More expansion and remodeling followed in 1928, when the building was sold to the Mills Building Corporation, which leased it back to the White House.

The Times gave a front page banner headline to the $1million deal which linked the White House and Mills Building. The store got more space out of the trade, extending its sales rooms all the way to Oregon Street.

Still other departments were added as the need for them became apparent. In 1933 the men's department became part of the store.

Greater expansion followed after World War II, when a $500,000 program was announced in 1946.

LONGEST ESCALATOR

Included in this was the $120,000 escalator which at that time was the longest single-span escalator in the United States. More space on the ground floor of the Mills Building also was acquired at this time for personnel offices, executive offices, business offices, credit offices and a beauty salon.

The second floor of the building was completely redecorated and a ladies' lounge was added. The first floor and mezzanine also were completely refixtured and remodeled.

Jack Miller, the delivery boy of 1900, had become president of the company in 1943 on the death of Myrtil Coblentz. Miller had worked as salesman and a window-trimmer, sign-writer, advertising man, floor-walker, general manager and vice-president, giving him an insight into every aspect of the business.

He also assumed a position as a civic leader, contributing much of his time to community projects.

Gaston Coblentz, brother of Myrtil, had died in 1942 in New York, where he spent most of his time in the buying end of the business.

A big addition to the White House's customer-popularity was made in 1949 when the company bought a parking lot on Main Street about two blocks from the store. A warehouse was acquired about the same time.

An appliance annex was added to the store, in the Oregon street side of the Mills Building, in 1951.

Jake Miller, after 12 years as president of the company, died in May, 1955, and was succeeded by his son, Dick, in the following month[11].

While the White House was very well known as a high end department store, the land upon which it was built had a long and interesting history as well.

The following is a clipping referring to the history of the location occupied by the White House.

1952: Old Central Hotel Built On Site Of Ponce De Leon's Ranch House

March 9, 1952

Bob Chapman

These were the days when Indians whooped it up in this area, the overland stage rattled into the village and Juan Maria Ponce de Leon moved in and set up his sprawling adobe ranch headquarters, extending all the way from the north side of Pioneer Plaza to Main Street.

---

[11] Tales From the Morgue, Trish Long, "Juarez Store founded In 1880 Became EP's Modern White House"

These are the scenes, incidents, atmosphere and color that make up the background of the old Central Hotel, first in the line of El Paso's famous hotels of yesteryears.

Time when Kingston, N.M., was a lively flourishing and prosperous mining camp also is a part of the story.

The Central, confused even by the few remaining old-timers with the Grand Central, which was on the present Mills Building site and whose frontage was on Oregon Street, stood where now is the White House Department Store, McCoy Hotel and Plaza Theater.

The Grand Central was destroyed by fire on Feb. 11, 1892. A fire, July 4, 1896, wiped out the Central.

REMEMBERS FIRE – Deputy Constable Fred Delgado, who came here from Fort Davis, Texas, in 1884, learned to be a tailor and, in 1892, was working for Jesus Teran, who had a tailor shop on the ground floor of the Central, remembered the fire but not is date. He recalled he was burned trying to save the tailor shop sign.

Delgado, who was born in Presidio, Texas, was a member of El Paso Police Department some 51 years ago.

A portion of the Ponce de Leon ranch house, built in 1827, served as both a apart of and the foundation for the Central Hotel, which, in the beginning, was a one-story affair. After the first Southern Pacific passenger train puffed into El Paso in 1881, a second story was added to the hotel. This was built of redwood lumber shipped in from California.

In an issue of The El Paso Times, Feb.6, 1937, in a column, whose heading was "Looking Back," there is a story dated Dec. 5, 1893, about Mrs. Elizabeth Gillock, who at the age of 94, died the preceding day in her home in Ysleta, Lower Valley.

FIRST HOTEL – This story recited that Mrs. Gillock kept the first hotel in El Paso and that hotel was the old Central, which was where the Plaza Theater now stands. The story also said it was a part of the Ponce de Leon ranch house.

Mrs. Gillock, according to this story, posted all delinquent accounts on a tree in Little Plaza (Pioneer Plaza). This, doubtless, was her way of publicizing guests who owed her money.

Without giving her name, the story quotes a woman who came here in 1873 to this effect: "Mrs. Gillock owned the hotel and land around it. Her trade was gone with the 49ers, so she lived in the rambling hotel all alone. It was of adobe and almost in ruins. When the railroads came she sold her property for $17,000, I think."

H. Y. Ellis, pioneer citizen, who came here in 1890 from Atlanta, Ga., with his father, Jesse M. Ellis, remembered the Central and the old red brick County Courthouse, scene of outstanding social events in those early days. Ellis said he attended many swanky dancing parties in that ancient structure.

FATHER WAS JP – His father was elected a justice of the peace in 1899 and served for four years. His court room was in the Bronson Block, present site of the American Furniture Co. building.

Ellis and his father slept in a room adjoining the court room. Ellis recalled lawyers had most of the offices in the building, R. C. Walshe being one.

Ellis joined El Paso Volunteer Firemen's Association in 1901. He is the current secretary, Ben Levy, another pioneer, is president.

Jake Miller, president of the White House Department Store, who came here in 1895, remembered the old Central and he fixed the date of the fire that destroyed it – July 4, 1896.

"I remembered that because there were a lot of fireworks exploding throughout the downtown area, as well as in the residential sections," Miller said.

NEWELLS ARRIVE – Enter now by a circuitous route Mr. and Mrs. George W. Newell, whose hometown, before they traveled west, was St. Louis, Mo. They landed first in Santa Fe, N.M. Mr. Newell was a hardware merchant and he opened a store there, operating this for two years.

The Newells had heard of increasing activities in the Kingston mining camp. So, the Santa Fe store was sold and they journeyed there.

Mrs. Newell, now past 82, said the same rock hotel where they first stayed, is still standing and carrying on.

"It was such a nice place," she said.

Mr. Newell set up a hardware store, which he ran for about two years. Mrs. Newell said he sold out just in time, because the bottom of the mining business started falling out.

"I hear this is picking up again," Mrs. Newell said. "I am glad. That is such a beautiful spot."

RODE IN STAGE COACH – Milton, the Newell's son born in Kingston, was 5-months old, when the stage coach drawn by four mules, pulled up and stopped in front of the rock hotel where the family was waiting for it. At Hillsboro, N.M., they changed into another stage coach, also pulled by four mules and jolted along to a railway station. Mrs. Newell could not recall the name.

It was 11 p.m. on a December night in 1892 when the train arrived in El Paso. Mrs. Newell said they stepped out of the train into a bitter cold, blinding snow storm. They got into a hack and started the hunt for a hotel room. It was a discouraging procedure.

There was an opera company in town, booked for the old Myar Opera House, and so hotels, in addition to their regular run of guests, had to take care of members of the opera cast.

Swirling snowflakes had grown larger and thicker by the time the hack halted at the Vendome Hotel, then on the present site of Hotel Cortez. Mr. Newell got out, went inside and returned with the dismal report the hotel was filled to overflowing.

BABY WON MANAGER – "We can't keep this baby out in this bitter weather," Mrs. Newell said. "Let me try and see what I can do about a place to stay."

Mrs. Newell took Milton inside. "Milton was such a happy, friendly baby," Mrs. Newell said. "When he gooed and gurgled at the manager, he said for us to come in, he would find a room."

Mrs. Newell could not remember the name of this manager, but she said he gave them his room and slept on a pallet in the parlor. (Parlor in those days. Not lobby.)

After being here several days, Mrs. Newell, taking Milton, went to St. Louis to visit her mother for three months. When she returned, Mr. Newell and a Mr. Gaston (initials not available) were in the grocery business on South El Paso Street. Mr. Newell was a hardware man. He didn't like selling groceries.

They sold the place and bought the lease on the hotel in the Center Block building, cornering on Pioneer Plaza and San Francisco Street. It was a three-story structure then. The hotel part was on the second and third floors. Mrs. Newell said it was beautifully furnished. In the corner, where now is one of the Oasis café, was a grocery store owned by Stuart and McNair. The store was sold to Charley Slack, E. A. Stuart moved to California and later organized the Carnation Milk Company.

PART OF THEATER – The present two-story building is part of the Plaza Theater property. Main entrance to the hotel was on San Francisco Street. The old Central Hotel backed up against the rear entrance, which then was in the vicinity of the north end of the Mills Restaurant and Confectionery.

Mrs. Newell recalled there was a Chinese restaurant at the east end of the Central. She remembered vividly the fire that left the Central a smoldering ruin, because volunteer fire fighters dragged hose through her hotel to battle the blaze from there. In their wake was considerably damaged furniture, fixtures and furnishings, she said.

The Newells had operated the hotel for about nine years when the building was sold. The third story was removed. Why, Mrs. Newell said she didn't know and couldn't guess.

BUILT HOME – Mr. Newell had bought property in the 100 block on West Franklin Street and built a home into which the family moved. Two other dwellings were added and a commercial garage at the corner of Franklin and North El Paso Street. Mrs. Newell lived in the dwelling at 110 West Franklin Street.

EXPANSION

As the White House store entered its 2nd decade, its popularity began to exceed its size. A new White House Department Store/McCoy Hotel bldg. was planned, then built on the site of the old Central Hotel (1881) owned by John Dougher[12], an immigrant from Ireland, the father of

---

[12] 1841-1888

Susie M. McCoy[13]. Mrs. McCoy ran the McCoy Hotel in this bldg. with husband William until she sold it in 1928, 3 yrs. after her husband died.

A "**Wait for the Opening**" ad campaign teased the upcoming launch of the new White House store, which was finally celebrated on Thursday night, 15 Mar, 1912 • describing the glitzy debut, El Paso historian **Leon Metz** wrote that "regally uniformed doormen assisted customers descending from their carriages."

"The young women employees of the 'White House' were most exquisitely gowned in white, with bouquets of flowers, and played hostesses in a charming manner[14]*."*

"The store also boasted a tea room run by the Potter Confectionery Company that sold French pastries, chocolates, sandwiches, salads, and coffee and tea. Adjoining the tea room were a rest room, the retiring room and a gold and white French parlor, designed especially for trying on clothes[15]."

In 1977, after the company had opened suburban branches, the downtown White House was shut down. The last remaining store in the chain closed its doors in 1983

---

[13] 1868-1948

[14] El Paso Herald, 15 Mar, 1912 p. 8

[15] El Paso Community College Libraries.

MILLS BUILDING

**303 N. Oregon
El Paso, Texas**

Figure 7: The Central Hotel with the Mills Building to the Right.

The **Anson Mills Building** is a historic building located at 303 North Oregon Street in El Paso, Texas. The building stands on the original site of the 1832 Ponce de León ranch.

Anson Mills hired Henry C. Trost of the Trost and Trost architectural firm to design and construct the building. Trost was the area's foremost pioneer in the use of reinforced concrete. Built in 1910-1911, the building was only the second concrete-frame skyscraper in the United States, and one of the largest all-concrete buildings. At 145 feet (44 m), the 12-story Mills Building was the tallest building in El Paso when completed. The architectural firm of Trost and Trost moved its offices to the building upon completion, where they remained until 1920.

The Mills family sold the building in 1965. The building stands on a corner site opposite San Jacinto Plaza, with a gracefully curved street facade that wraps around the south and east sides. Like many of Trost's designs, the Anson Mills Building's overall form and strong verticality, as well as details of the ornamentation and cornice, are reminiscent of the Chicago School work of Louis Sullivan.

Downtown El Paso has a jaw-dropping collection of historic buildings. Look above the first-floor retail alterations and you'll see untouched wood windows, intricate plasterwork, colorful tile, and strong masses of concrete and brick. Fine architecture was a point of personal and civic pride. This is the downtown that was and the downtown that could be. One building that has returned to its former glory is the Anson Mills Building.

Anson Mills was just 23 years old when he first saw El Paso in 1858. Though Paso del Norte on the Mexican side of the river was a sizable and prosperous town, the Texas side consisted of a ranch and a post office bearing the name Franklin. Former West Point classmates were stationed at nearby Fort Bliss, and with their recommendation, Mills was appointed surveyor for the district. He platted the town and changed its name from Franklin to El Paso. By surveying the land for 200 miles south of El Paso and building homes and stagecoach stations, Mills was able to acquire his own land. But his

rising fortunes changed when he voted against secession. He left for Washington, D.C., and didn't see El Paso again for 20 years.

After fighting for the Union in the Civil War, Mills served

Figure 8:Colonel Anson Mills

in the Army throughout the West and the Great Plains, eventually rising to the rank of Brigadier General. He spent more than 50 years in the military, and was stationed at Fort Bliss several times. As Commissioner of the International Boundary Commission, he spent 20 years negotiating the Mexico-U.S. boundary of the ever-changing Rio Grande and advocated equitable distribution of water from the Colorado and New Mexico headwaters of the river. During his lifetime, El Paso grew from a bucolic ranch to a city of more than 50,000 people.

The Anson Mills Building in downtown El Paso recently completed its final review for the Federal Historic Preservation Tax Incentives.

By 2007, the building was covered with dingy brown paint. Decades before, bronze mirrored glass windows had replaced the original windows, and those bronze windows were pockmarked with plywood covers. The interior of the building had been gutted by previous owners. Still, the remarkable 12-story concrete structure was in good condition. The owners of **Mills Plaza Properties** saw the potential of the building and recognized the possibility of using the Federal Historic Preservation Tax Incentives to rehabilitate it.

Now, new windows match the appearance of the original windows. A stair and elevator tower was built in the alley area. Large openings were cut along the walls on the entire western face of the building. An addition extended the full height of the building along the west side.

An open-air passageway between the Mills and White House Department Store was enclosed for a new corridor. The parking and commercial structure adjacent to the Mills Building is based on the appearance of the St. Regis Hotel that occupied that location long ago. Additions are visible, but they are set back and on non-primary facades. The alterations and additions were necessary to make the building rentable and to generally revitalize it. The exterior was painted a light taupe, with a darker taupe for the accent color.

The Anson Mills Building now features the popular Anson 11 restaurant on the 1st and 2nd floors, with office tenants on the upper floors. It's a fine example of how the tax credits can be used to rehabilitate historic buildings. "We are very proud of what we were able to do to bring back its original glory," said Brent Harris of Mills Plaza Properties.

Before the renovation, the building looked very much like a movie version of a haunted building. Homeless who used to spend their nights in San Jacinto Plaza talked of seeing figures moving behind the dingy windows and hearing faint screams.

International Business College (IBC) used to have their main offices and campus in the Mills Building. A former secretary to the president of IBC discussed some of her interactions with the unknown. She talked about coming in on the weekends to catch up on her paperwork. She talked to hearing movement in the corridors and smelling smoke at a time she was the only person in the building. She would run out into the corridors and see figures in nightclothes round the curve of the corridors. Though she gave chase, she never found anyone in the building.

EL PASO PUBLIC LIBRARY

501 N. Oregon Street
El Paso, Texas

Figure 9: El Paso Public Library

In early 1884, the women of El Paso came together in order to organize a library and reading room for El Paso. However, it was not until 1894 that Mary Stanton, a local teacher organized the first reading club for boys with some 600-800 books from her own personal library. The reading club was established in the Sheldon Building and the key to the room was given to the elevator operator. The boys who were members would get the key from the elevator operator, let themselves in and keep track of circulation. By 1895, the reading club was open to anyone who could pay a twenty-five cent membership fee and donate one standard periodical a month or, in lieu of donating a periodical, pay a fifty cent membership fee. From this start, the first library association was opened in 1896 and Ms. Stanton became the librarian. In 1899, the library moved into the newly completed City Hall.

In 1902, Andrew Carnegie gave $35,000.00 to the City of El Paso for a library building and the City Council voted an annual tax to support the library. The new building was erected on Buckler Square, bounded by Oregon, Missouri, El Paso and Franklins Streets. The new facility, constructed in a classic revival style opened on April 25, 1904, but in less than fifteen years was judged hopelessly inadequate for the City's needs. In 1919, a second floor was added and outdoor reading rooms were added to address the overcrowding. Continued improvements were made to the building, but no one believed that this was a long term solution. Finally, in 1951, voters approved a $975,000.00 bond issue for the construction of a new facility to house the ever growing library. The new building was designed by the architectural firm of Carroll and Daeuble. The new library opened in 1954. The land upon which the library sits was also the site of El Paso's first cemetery. When it became obvious that the land would be needed for building, the town drunks were hired to dig up all of the interred bodies and move them to Concordia Cemetery. But not everybody was moved.

The floor upon which one enters the Public Library is actually the third floor of the building. There are two floors below ground level housing achieves and governmental records. Access to the other floors is via a narrow winding stair case or elevator. There have been one or two strange encounters on this elevator that are worthy of note. When I mentioned to some friends that I was going to write about the ghosts at the Public Library, one mentioned something that had happened to a friend of hers. It was almost closing and her friend was rushing to check out some books when the elevator doors opened. Standing just inside the doors was a lady wearing an old timey nurse's uniform. She said the nurse looked confused, and kept glancing around as if expecting someone. Finally, the doors closed. When the doors opened a minute later, though the indicator had not shown the car moving, the car was empty.

Others have encountered the ghostly nurse. The Heritage Tourism Guide of The El Paso Scene for April 2000 reported that a maintenance worker on the main floor walked past the stair case and glanced down the stairs. He saw, standing on the landing for the first basement level, a woman dressed in an old time nurses' uniform wearing a cape. She was standing looking up the stairs toward him. He had taken a couple of steps past the stairwell before he realized what he had seen and he went back. She was gone.

Two other library employees were waiting for the elevator one evening. When the car opened, there was a young man standing in the car, facing the back wall. The man was wearing a dark coat and no hat. Before the two could enter the car, the doors closed and then opened almost immediately, the car was empty.

Other spirits include a Confederate soldier who has been seen reading on the first floor and an invisible typist. There is a ghost, thought to be female, which knocks books off of the shelves in the Government section on the second basement level. This second basement level is also where an employee saw a huge Black man dressed in the style of the 1920s wearing muddy boots, frantically searching the shelves in one section of the library. When he realized he had been seen, he looked at the employee, down at his muddy boots and then he left via an exit. When the employee reached where the man had been standing there was no sign of water or mud on the floor, but there was no doubt that the boots had been muddy. Who was he and what was he searching for?

On the first level is the "Colonel's" chair, originally part of the Burgess House furnishings. The "Colonel" placed the chair where he wanted it and if anyone moved it, the chair would be found back in the original location. Figures have been seen in areas that are off limits to the public, but when security searches, there is never anyone found. The sounds of a typist are heard as well the creaking sounds of old style wooden chairs in areas where there are no people. An electrician got the shock of his life when he was working on a light fixture and saw a face reflected in it of someone behind him. When he looked around no one was there. As with so many other locations in El Paso, the motion sensors are set off so often that it takes a unique event for security to open the locked building to conduct a search.

And if these ghosts are not enough, consider what happened to Ms. Terry Grant. Ms. Grant works in the Border Heritage Center of the El Paso Public Library. She is a Library Information Specialist II. She was working one Sunday night when she had a first-hand experience with the entities that she had long heard inhabit the building. On that Sunday night as she was preparing to close, she heard a rustling of papers from a corner of the Border Heritage Center that cannot be ready seen due to a row of filing cabinets. Thinking a patron was still in that out of the way corner, she started to walk around the row of cabinet. To her surprise, she felt something push against her chest as she rounded the corner; something that would not let her go behind those filing cabinets. Quickly she summoned a co-worker and asked him to go check that corner of the room. Obligingly, he walked past the file cabinets and all was quiet for a few minutes and then he came shooting out of that isolated corner heading for the door. He told her that he had felt resistance to his entry, but once he had moved passed the cabinets, he felt as if the walls were closing in and he saw that the sign that sat in the middle of the table was moving. At that point he decided it was time to leave.

The El Paso Public Library has enough hauntings and strange events to warrant a book all its own. What I have outlined here merely scratches the surface. But if I have given you to idea that the Library isn't just for books any more, than I have accomplished my purpose.

FIRST CHRISTIAN CHURCH

**500 Oregon
El Paso, Texas**

Across the street from the Public Library is 500 N. Oregon, a building

Figure 10: Building that housed the First Christian Church.

about which numerous stories are told. Originally built to house the First Christian Church, this building now sits forlorn and, for the most part, empty. The First Christian Church now occupies the entire 900 Block on Arizona Street. However, this was not always the case. In 1883, Philip Miner, a blacksmith, and his family moved to El Paso[16]. By day, he worked at his forge, but in the evening, Mr. Miner could be found praying and teaching the gospels to a few disciples who he gathered together.

In 1885, the little group, that had grown to include thirteen members, became an organized congregation, even though it had nowhere to meet. Not letting a little thing like no place to meet stop them, the little group showed they could be very resourceful in finding places in which they could practice their religion. This group included Millard Patterson, James A Ashford, Zeno B. Clardy, William Coldwell, H.F. Sanders, Claude Miner, Emma Miner, Susie Brack, Mrs. Robert F. Campbell, Mrs. A. J. Stevens, Miss Linder Moyer, Mrs. E. C. Pew and the Reverend Miner.

They met first in the small adobe house at First and Stanton Street, then in the District Court Room, then in a building on Campbell Street that was also used by the post office and then in a paint shop on Stanton Street. Finally, they obtained a building at 107 Myrtle Avenue. Unfortunately, this first building was sold in 1903, but in January 1904, ground was broken for a brick building at the

---

[16] Jones, Harriot Howze, El Paso: A Centennial Report, A Project of the El Paso County Historical Society, Superior Printing, Inc., El Paso, Texas 1972.

corner of Oregon and Franklin Streets. This building served as the church building until the new, larger church building was opened in 1952. The building actually faces Oregon, but its' length runs along Franklin. The picture above shows the Franklin Street side of the building. As can be seen, since the First Christian Church moved the new owners have divided the building and rented to a number of tenants.

I talked to Derrell Hiett, Director of the International Art Museum and who used to be partners with the owner of Baron's Primitive Indian Artifacts, who had his business in this building for six or seven years. During slow periods, they would explore the building. In the basement area there a tunnel that runs underneath Franklin Street to the south. It is bricked up now, but it is possible to see where the entrance to the tunnel was located. Mr. Hiett said that in the basement he would always feel strange, as if someone was watching him. Strange sounds were heard and figures seen. There was definitely something unusual about the basement area.

CHASE TOWER

201 East Main
El Paso, Texas

Figure 11: The entrance to the El Paso Club, 18th Floor of the Chase Bank Building[17].

In my first book, *Spirits of the Border: The History and Mystery of El Paso Del Norte[18]*, I wrote about the

---

[17] This photo is from the author's collection.
TP[18]PT Hudnall, Ken and Connie Wang, The Spirits of the Border: The History and Mystery of El Paso Del Norte, Omega Press, El Paso, Texas. 2003.

Chase Bank Building at 210 E. Main Street. I didn't have much at the time, merely the story of a woman in a red dress being seen on the top floor and strange lights being seen late at night.

I now have more information on this haunting. I had occasion to speak to a group at the El Paso Club, an eating establishment which occupies the top floor of the Chase Bank Building Tower.

Figure 12: The Chase bank Tower, which dominates the El Paso skyline.

I was discussing the ghosts of El Paso and then discussed the ghost of the woman in the red dress that haunts the El Paso Club and made a comment that they should be watching for that particular ghost. At that point, one of the members of the group who had been sitting quietly listening suddenly called the waiter over to his table and asked him if he had ever seen a ghost during the time that he had been working at the El Paso Club.

To everyone's surprise, the waiter confirmed that he had seen the ghost in the red dress. He said that some evenings he and others working there had seen a pretty lady in a red dress enter the dining room in which we were eating. She looked as real as anyone else and would generally go over to stare out the windows that looked toward the east. However, if anyone approached her or tried to speak to her, the woman would fade away.

He also went on to say that some nights when they were there late cleaning up from the evening's business, they would hear the glasses at the bar clinking as if someone was making a drink and sometimes they would hear what sounded like a large group of people talking elsewhere in the restaurant. The voices were normally pitched so low that while the sound of conversation could be heard, the actual words could not be understood.

He also confirmed that late some evenings if he happened to be in sight of the building, he could sometimes see what looked like lights burning in the Club at times he knew that the El Paso Club was empty.

THE CORTEZ BUILDING

310 N. Mesa
El Paso, Texas

Figure 13: The Cortez Building (Hotel Vendome)

Located on the northeast corner of North Mesa Street and Mills Avenue, the 11-story Cortez Building began its life as the Hotel Vendome, El Paso's oldest hotel. The structure takes the shape of an L-shaped block about the second story, with twelve bays facing Mesa and ten bays facing Mills[19]. While this building was never ranked as one of Trost's more artistic designs, it did incorporate one original feature not found in other buildings of the period. Peering out of the roundels above the Mesa Street entrance is a series of portrait heads of conquistadors[20].

The hotel was erected at a cost of $1,500,000.00 for Alzina Orndorff de Groff, a hotel operator in Tucson and El Paso. This new hotel, to be called the Hotel Orndorff, was the third hotel to bear that name and the second Orndorff Hotel to occupy that same spot of land. It has been said that between the cost of building the hotel and the rich furnishings that Alzina Orndorff de Groff spent $6,000,000.00[21].

One week before the opening of the grand Orndorff Hotel in 1926, Alzina Orndorff de Groff was caught in a freak rainstorm, came down with pneumonia and died before the grand opening so had so looked forward to. Even so, it is said by some that she still watches over her dream hotel. Changes are unwelcome in this hotel.

---

[19] Jones, Harriot Howze, El Paso: A Centennial Report, A Project of the El Paso County Historical Society, Superior Printing Inc, Texas 1972.
[20] There is a belief that one of the heads decorating the front of the building is that of Henry Trost.
[21] Ligon, III, Andrew J. Haunting behind Scenes: Cultural Sports Grapple With Ghosts, El Paso Herald Post, October 31, 1996.

In the lobby, workers have maintained that they feel the presence of others even when they are alone and most feel that these presences come and go up and down the stairs. There have been reports of reflections of people being seen in the gleaming metal work of the elevators who are not in the elevators.

Connie Wang used to go through the building with the El Paso Ghost Tour and was very friendly with the security guard. One day she saw him walk past her without speaking and round the corner in one of the halls. She followed him to see if something was wrong, but when she rounded the corner, only seconds later, the hallway was empty, she found out later that he had not been at work that day, he was home ill. So what or who had she seen?

Children have been seen and heard playing in the hallways when there are no children in the building. How about Joseph, the little boy who loves to ride his cycle in the lobby area. If approached he will race around the corner and vanish, much the same way as the guard Connie Wang saw.

There was once a fast food restaurant located in one of the retail areas of the building. The night crew would complain of people coming to the counter, placing and order and then vanishing when the worker turned to fill the order. I am told that some employees refused to work the night shift.

In the ballroom of this grand building, a young woman dressed in a ball gown from another era sitting weeping, but if she is approached she rises and walks into the shadows where there is no doorway, but she disappears. Was this perhaps once a doorway that is no more? It has been theorized that at this location there is a portal to another dimension where once wedding and parties were held. Perhaps some of these entities are caught in between worlds, so to speak, doomed forever to try and get back to their home but always failing. There are reports of a room off of the cloakroom where there seems to be some type of portal or energy vortex. Several psychics have called this a doorway, but a doorway to where?

POPULAR DEPARTMENT STORE
1 UNION FASHION CENTER
102 North Mesa Street
El Paso, Texas

This building was another that was designed by Henry C. Trost, using all white terra-cotta. It was built on the site of the old Masonic Building.

The Popular Dry Goods Company (known as The Popular and by its large Spanish-speaking clientele as La Popular) was a local chain of department stores in El Paso, Texas. It carried national brands of clothing, footwear, bedding, furniture, jewelry, beauty products, electronics, and housewares. At the time of its closing in 1995, there were four locations in El Paso at Downtown, Bassett Center, Northpark Mall and Sunland Park Mall. For much of its existence, The Popular was El Paso's largest locally owned department store.

The Popular Dry Goods Company was founded in 1902 by Adolf Schwartz, a Hungarian immigrant who had previously opened two other retail stores in the area, Tres B (Buena, Bonita, Barata/Good, Pretty, Cheap) and The Fair which he had founded in 1900. Schwartz closed The Fair in 1902 and it was succeeded by The Popular, which he opened with his nephew Maurice Schwartz and other relatives. In 1907, the Popular moved from the northeast corner of El Paso and Overland Streets to Mesa and San Antonio and consisted of three floors by 1914.

Completed in 1911 for Adolph Schwartz, the new building was built specifically to house the Popular Dry Goods Company that Schwartz had founded in 1902. The Popular, as it was known had first been located at South El Paso and Overland Streets and then it had moved over to occupy the Old Masonic Building. Finding that he needed more room and wanting a distinctive look, Schwartz turned to Trost who used the Chicago Commercial Style in arriving at an easily recognizable design for this dynamic company. For over 93 years, The Popular has served the region, only recently falling victim to declining markets.

In 1917 Schwartz transformed The Popular from a general store to a modern department store with a six-story building on Mesa and San Antonio Streets.

Schwartz's granddaughter Ann Goodman Schaechner, tells a story about Pancho Villa and Francisco Madero, opposing military leaders in the Mexican Revolution, visiting The Popular at the same time, "One was on the basement and the first floor and the other was on the second or third floor. A clerk recognized the foes and ran back and forth between floors attending the two men so that they would not bump into each other. Thanks to the observant employee, the two men never saw each other, and the store kept both good customers."

Adolph Schwartz died from a heart attack at the age of 74 on March 3, 1941. After the retirement of Schwartz' nephew Maurice, Maurice's sons Herbert M. Schwartz and Albert J. Schwartz, continued to run the company.

The Popular's expansion began in 1962 with the opening of a second location at Bassett Center. This was followed by a third location at Northgate (later Northpark Mall) in 1966, and then a location at Sunland Park Mall in 1987.

In 1995, the devalued peso and Mexico's recession along with the newly enacted North American Free Trade Agreement posed an economic strain to the region. All Popular stores were closed on November 6, 1995. Dillard's purchased The Popular's credit accounts and Bassett Center store. Sears purchased the Sunland Park location. The remaining two locations were dissolved.

Though this building has seen a resurrection as a department store as Union Fashion, it would seem from some of the stories that I have heard that some of the older customers of the former Popular Department Store have no intention of leaving. The elevators respond to calls on the upper floors when there is no one in the building. Doors are heard to slam, voices are heard in empty rooms and footsteps are heard by employees when they are the only ones in the room.

Then there are the stories associated with the basement area. According to one of the workers, some days when the work crew would go into the basement, a little boy wearing jeans and tennis shoes would jump out of the shadows, yell boo and then run laughing into the shadowy recesses of the basement area. No matter how thoroughly they would search, however, they could never find the little boy.

There is a related tale from the late 1940s that a mother came to the Popular to go shopping with her little boy. As the mother shopped, the little boy was free to wander about the aisles of the department store. When it came time for the mother to leave, she was unable to find her child and no matter how thoroughly they searched neither could the staff at the large department store. According to the mother, when he was last seen, her son was wearing jeans and tennis shoes. Could the two stories be related?

EPILOGUE

So this is the history and mystery tour that I have given to hundreds of people for over twenty years. Where most people see closed up, rundown buildings, for those aware of the colorful history, there is a mystique of romance and mystery. Downtown El Paso still hides many mysteries that will never be solved.

Watch for the next in the History and Mystery series dealing with other haunted locations in El Paso and other tours designed to delight and mystify.

INDEX

CPSIA information can be obtained
at www.ICGtesting.com
Printed in the USA
LVHW022328220920
666821LV00006B/915